CW01594504

TRIUMPH HOUSE
Poetry with a Purpose

ARISE FROM THE SHADOWS

Edited by

Steve Twelvetree

First published in Great Britain in 2001 by
TRIUMPH HOUSE
Remus House,
Coltsfoot Drive,
Peterborough, PE2 9JX
Telephone (01733) 898102

HB ISBN 1 86161 854 9
SB ISBN 1 86161 859 X

FOREWORD

Throughout our lives we all experience times of despair and discomfort. Whether it be through grief, dismay, anger or frustration; by looking at the lighter side of life we can overcome these darker days.

Over 100 new and established authors have come together in this touching anthology to create a selection of messages to those in need of inspiration. Each poem differs in both style and content and has its own unique message of hope and faith.

You are sure to be enlightened by this genuinely comforting and uplifting collection of verse. So read on and experience all this anthology has to offer.

Steve Twelvetree
Editor

CONTENTS

CAST A DARK SHADOW

In the pale eye of dawn lies
a long dark shadow.
Somewhere, a child cries. Somewhere,
beneath the debris of war,
a child lies. Somewhere, a hand
reaches out. Somewhere, a child dies.

In the pale eye of dawn lies
a long dark shadow.
Somewhere, a siren calls. Somewhere,
beneath the underbelly of war,
a bomb falls. Somewhere, a man
voices an order. Somewhere, a man dies.

And in the pale eye of the world lies
a long dark shadow.
Somewhere, war casts a long dark
shadow of death, of destruction,
of annihilation, of anger: of fear. And
somewhere a child cries and somewhere
a child dies: until somewhere an eye
shifts focus and a hand reaches out for peace.

Jocelyn McKinnon

To You My Chant

Nations of hundreds of creeds
Have been called to witness
The greatest sacrifice
From Thee Greatest of Men

Though many weren't believers
He surrendered to them all
Engraving His sacred Sign
For the cycles of the centuries

Oh sublime sacred 'Logos'!
Symbol of deliverance and power
Exalted to a Divine Covenant
Out of persecution and suffer

Venerated Holy 'Logos'
Pardon death and resurrection
Fountain of encouragement
Healer of passions . . . Giver of love

'Logos' of the poor and the rich
Emblem of what forever last
Fluttering swallow into the sun
Nourishment to all living light

Road to our bodies and souls
Solace to our sorrows and hopes
    Celestial helping hand
Oasis to our wonder and roam

Peace to our tormented nights
Beauty to our forthcoming days
Only trust . . . Only baptism
    Fulfilment to our cry

My quest in Your presence ends
You are my flag; Freedom is mine
Threshold to my heritage
Majestic Eternal Christ

Eduardo Del-Rio Escalona

HUMANITY

When you wake up from your slumber and clamber out of bed,
Think on how to start your day and remember things I've said.
Life is but our lesson and we are here to live and learn
Sharing our joy and knowledge, compassion and concern.

It is not always easy to accept the challenge that life doth hold,
And brave the lashings of the storm so bitter, sad and cold
But when the showers of tears are over and you come out to the sun
You will feel the rays of happiness and the joy that is to come.

Each one of us is special and plays a part towards mankind,
Always leaving something somewhere for loved ones left behind.
So don't impose your will on others, listen to what they say,
Let tolerance and patience guide you through each day.

Accept your sister and your brother, with all their faults and fears,
You must learn to share together, your laughter and your tears.
Do not take this all for granted for they are not always there,
Make the most of every moment and show how very much you care.

Anne Eycott

THE SACRIFICE

A silence settled all around
   As moonlight filtered on the ground,
Those ghostly figures lying there
   Were scattered lifeless everywhere

Yet just a few hours ago
   Their youth and strength were in full flow,
They viewed tomorrow as secure,
   In spite of what they might endure

They rested in the cold, damp air,
   Within each face a vacant stare
Their youth was gone forever now
   And duty touched each death-white brow

The countryside was strewn with holes,
   Accepting all the murdered souls
Like open graves before the prayer,
   Which left them to another's care

A distant sky revealed the dawn,
   The blood-red light had come to mourn
Those young men who were someone's son,
   Now lost souls gone beyond the sun

Then through the mist the stretchers came,
   To lift those bodies lost to fame
And carry them towards the hill,
   Their Calvary, though cold and chill

Those pure white crosses stand there now,
   And every year mothers ask how
Their sons were sacrificed this way,
   And then they slowly walk away.

Douglas Thomas

RESTORATION

After destruction and desolation
Branches are bare
The air is quiet
The lull is here

The locusts have gone
Barrenness of pain remains
Can restoration come?
Healing of spring.

'I will restore the years
The locusts have eaten'
Says the Lord

The spirit comes
He reveals and heals
He plants new seeds
New buds to form.

His Grace waters the dried earth
Open to receive
Be anointed
Recreation begins

'I will restore the years
The locusts have eaten'
Says the Lord

God's forgiveness and mercy
Restores my soul
As barren branches
Break forth in their beauty

Arms, branches, rising up
Fingers, leaves opening
Eyes open wide
Creation in bloom

Beth Powney

Candle In The Dark

That ray of hope in the midnight hour
A tiny spark
Timeless essence of the night
Flickering shadows from incandescent light.

An illuminating warmth
Drawing kindred spirits
The candle burning bright

A contrast of love and fear
Symbol of peace and unity
What does it represent to you

Angels tread on the lighted path
Soothing our souls with gracious meditation
A multitude of joyful thoughts
Fulfilling our being

In the stillness of the night
I can see the light
It sheds its rays on my path

I follow it
And in my wake
Know where it will lead me at last . . .

Christine Jackson

Stay With Me

You touched
My heart
From the start,
Allowing
Me to shine,
Happiness
You gave to me
Contentment
All the time,
Never
Am I lonely,
Life is
So divine,
Knowing
You're beside me
Guide me
To your light,
Choices, that I make
Decisions, on my mind,
Help me
With some answers
Difficult to find,
Things I cannot see
I pray
When I am blind
Feeling you
A presence
Showing me a sign.

Martin Toyne

THE WARD AT NIGHT

The ward is silent,
It is night;
There is darkness,
Not much light!

Some are moaning,
As they sleep;
Others snore,
In slumber deep!

The monitors,
So softly tick;
As Nursing staff
Attend the sick!

The 'Graveyard Shift'
Is passing - slow!
But when dawn comes,
The sun will glow!

A 'Beeper' sounds!
A nurse comes fast!
A false alarm!
The danger's past!

No panic then,
And no 'Code Blue'!
A simple need,
A portaloo!

Ron Bissett

We Shall Reap

Do we sow with a view to be kind - do we find words to
use that are uplifting as we speak - that has the power to
lift the saddened spirit of another human soul - dwelling on this
earth - are we always ready to offer a hand - when there is an
honest need - all helping to make our world a better place to both
live and dwell - or are we short-sighted - holding back a kind
spoken word - even turn our face not to see the real need - offering
no hand of friendship to ones that have a need - then true to the
written word - we all must reap what we have sown in our
passing life - keeping in mind God is not one to be mocked - his
searching eyes can see what is happening on this globe - and he will
hold each one of us to full account - then shall we still continue
in our wrong ways - or shall we try to make amends helping to
make the world a better place to live and dwell - man at this time is
troubled in so many ways - around the globe - both hate and greed seem
to rule the day that is until the very heavens cry out enough
enough - it will be a time when all mankind must feel
ready to face a judgement day when all will reap
what they have sown - Amen.

R P Scannell

A Prayer For Monkia

(A prayer written to a sister on the anniversary of the death of her husband)

Your sister and your brother too
Remember this, the fateful day
Your husband Gilles, whom we all loved
Was taken from us, far away.

Dear Monika, we're at your side,
Remembering this lovely guy,
Who brought great joy to everyone
He touched in life, as he passed by.

We know so will the grief remains,
We know how bravely you face life
Without your consort, all alone,
Yet knowing that you have God's love.

You know that God is on your side
To help you build your life anew;
Belief in Whom has seen you through
Such grief, assured His love is true.

Oh Lord, where would we be today
Were You not ever there to turn to?
The comfort we receive through prayer
Revives our minds and spirits anew.

Christopher Head

PRAY WITH ONE ANOTHER - THAT YOU MAY BE HEALED

Jesus - where are you?
Why don't you come when I call?
I hate this silence
- the feeling of total isolation.

I stretch out my hands to reach you,
to sense your presence
and to bask in your love
but the coldness and darkness
extinguishes all hope.

I am alone. Totally alone.
I sit in the darkness grieving and mourning
For your presence again.

Then - you carry me out of the darkness
through my brothers and sisters.
Physically you comfort me,
spiritually you feed me,
and as they weep with me and pray with me
their love becomes - you.
Gradually, the dying flame flickers
and my heart warms within me.
As I look up you greet me
and the warmth of your love
and the tenderness of your smile
gives me hope to carry on.
Praise God!

Linda Fawkes

Empty Spaces

At first the empty spaces seem like gaping holes,
Only little comfort comes from watching burning coals,
The armchair looks so empty and somehow so cold,
It should be filled with the person you so dearly want to hold.

Sit in the chair and feel the times you both have loved to share,
Remember as you sit and think the person, who was there,
The times you laughed, the things you've done and planned together,
The children and the animals those memories last forever.

Then soon the empty spaces become times to reminisce,
Think of all the happy times and a smile won't seem amiss,
At times it can be good to cry and leave a space to pray,
The hurt just doesn't disappear but slowly fades away.

Time makes the empty spaces slowly begin to fill,
With people, places, experience, time refuses to stand still,
The empty spaces then get smaller and sad days are further apart,
The last and only empty space will always be in your heart.

A T Giddings

HALLMARKS OF LIFE

All God's children of this great wide world: His black, white, red and yellow too
Form a worldwide club of brotherhood, and help life's garden flower anew:
Heel in evergreens of kindliness; set corms of care; and plants of love
Sprinkle then fat seeds of tenderness, to tempt to Earth dear peaceful's dove.

All God's children of this great wide world; the rich, the poor, the young and old;
Form a worldwide club of brotherhood; shake freedom's flag from out its fold;
High then hold it up with mighty pride; for 'tis a joyous flag to see;
Each woven picture telling stories, of how God wants His world to be.

All God's children of this great wide world; from John-o' Groats to Timbuktu
From a worldwide club of brotherhood: all men make equal unto you;
Share with them your great technology; build not one hope on shifting sand;
Let all now reap your knowledge blossoms; in every parched and barren land.

All God's children of this great wide world; the bold; the mighty; and the strong.
Form a worldwide club of brotherhood; help weak and helpless souls along.
Proudly wear love's badge upon your breast, with F H C engraved in gold.
Faith, hope and blessed charity, the hallmarks stamped on life's great mould.

All God's children of this great wide world; compose right now a
joyful song;
With willing hearts to ever sing it; throughout the night and
all day long.
Silver chords that tell of rightfulness; of justice, truth and honesty.
Let heartbeats make the thankful music, to God's sweet love, eternally.

Violet M Corlett

One-Way Road

I got a wee shock.
When I heard the other day.
Old Mister so and so,
Had gone and passed away.

Looking round the neighbours,
People that we know,
You never know the minute.
When one of them will go.

Nothing we can do,
And not a thing to say,
It comes to everyone of us,
We cannot run away.

Funny thing, this life of ours.
It's the thing we want to keep.
No one that I know of.
Wants to take that last big sleep.

But sleep, like death, must claim us,
There is nothing we can do.
No one leaves this world alive,
And that, my friends is true.

But all is not lost,
If you kneel down and pray,
As God for forgiveness,
Please ask him today.

Now ask him to show you,
To light up the way,
How to get into Heaven,
The next time you pray.

J Moffett

SMILER

Give thought to all you have and smile,
Love life and give thanks, it only lasts a while.
You have your health, legs, arms, senses and brain,
Our coughs and colds cause minimal pain.
So be a *smiler be positive.*

Smile if you can walk around,
What you've lost can be found.
You can listen to music enjoy TV
Here at least most, of us can afford some tea.
We can make a choice 'That's for me!'
So Smile, be grateful, *happy with all you have.*

Happy because your pains are small,
So many people have no mobility at all.
From a wheelchair, they face hostility and fear,
Their possibility's little, as they shed a tear
While longingly wishing to burst into song,
Wanting no pity, they strive to get along.
Watching and waiting, to fit in and belong.
However life is at this moment in time,
Put a Smile on your face, and let your countenance shine.

Louise White

HELP (SOS)

Has life become empty, you just don't care,
Feel life's not worth living, it's so unfair,
For some have plenty but unwilling to share,
And living through life's no certain affair,
When you're feeling alone, unable to bear,
Pitching and tossing on a sea of despair
While sailing a ship that's going nowhere.
If that's how you feel, you'd better beware
For the devil may have you caught in his snare,
Enticing you in to live in his lair
And in so doing your life to impair.
So don't let that happen be strong and forbear,
Just cry out to God your life to impair.
And then you will find you've become aware
He's been travelling with you across L'mer
And patiently waiting your love to declare,
So give Him a signal, send up that flare -
Ask Him for mercy and offer your prayer,
Then a safe haven for you He'll prepare,
To His Kingdom of Heaven He'll make you an heir.

P J Tucker

When I Was Down He Helped Me

My life was full of dark despair
There seemed no point at all
In carrying on the struggle
As on each mountain climbed I'd fall

Each day a new knock put me down
There seemed no end to pain
Then suddenly through the torment
Once more came love again

But this love came from Jesus
Who in his wisdom saw my grief
And sent his faithful servants
To offer me kind relief

And when I saw the kindness offered
And the joy with which it was given
I knew then my life had been a test
From which the sad times now were driven

My life then changed from that day forth
For now I know that people care
From the simple words as told to me
'For you we said a prayer'

Don Woods

For You, For Me

Why do you wail, O Christian soul?
Your Saviour, Christ, has made you whole.
By dying on that shameful tree
He bought new life for you, for me.

Now by His stripes we both are healed,
His crimson blood has set, congealed.
His wounds, so terribly applied,
Show clearly how our Saviour died.

But not in vain, no, not in vain,
Goes out that challenging refrain,
His sacrifice is now complete,
Come, gather at the Saviour's feet.

Yesterday, today and on,
The ages roll, and soon are gone.
His love for us, both great and small,
Will never let God's children fall.

We can be sure that we shall see
Our Saviour in eternity,
We have His word that He will not
Forget His promise, not one jot.

Such love assures us that we count,
In valley or on steepest mount,
Where e'er we go, what e'er we do,
We know our Lord will see us through.

And this great love, so full, so free,
Our Lord pours out on you and me,
From all the riches of His dower,
Encapsuled in His grace and power.

Keith Allison

WALK IN THE SUN

I wish you could walk in the sun Mother
And feel the warmth on your face,
I wish you could walk in the sun Mother
With all your style and grace.

I wish you could feel the wind Mother
To cool your furrowed brow,
I wish you could feel the rain Mother
So you won't feel so low.

I wish you could dance again mother
With Dad as once you did,
And see you smile as once you could
When I was just a kid.

Could you but smell the fresh sea air,
As you did so long ago,
As we walked the Gower coastline
Along that sandy shore!

I wish you could stand again mother
And leave your chair behind,
Why did it happen to you mother?
You are so good and kind.

One day you will walk again Mother
With green grass 'neath your feet!
In a land of milk and honey
In a glorious retreat!

Derek J Morgan

JUST LIKE ME

Just like me,
you didn't know His strength
never perceived He walked that length
did care, did die, did rise, divineth

just like me,
you found out in pain
His blood to be our new life's gain
was this love, a freedom, could we be sane?

just like me,
you felt the touch of compassion
moved in the beat of breath's salvation
gave into the eyes that melted devastation,

just like me,
it cradled in love's empowering grace
of a hunger for peace, His peace
we breathed Him name to never cease

just like me,
you broke in His remaking,
endless tears mixing joy's understanding
saw new heavens a future so waiting

yes, just like each other
we know His name calms
we are lifted gently in Holy arms
knowing our hearts be safe in Him *scared* palms.

Linda Daly

Is There Anybody There

Help is there anybody there
To offer a listening ear
To show to us such tender care
To make us feel that he is near
However depressing life seems to be
And how much the future seems unclear
There's always joy when he is near
Christ truly sets us free.

I lift my hands to the King of Kings
And praise his holy name
Jesus said he could do all things
If only we believe
A window may close; life often deals blows
Christ lights the way - He'll open the door
And be our strength forever more
He'll help us along from day to day
He'll never go away.

Anthony Gibson

Peace And Resignation

We brought them out to Lourdes last year,
Two broken hearts, with many a tear,
The awful loneliness and pain,
Our lives would never be the same.
We saw his face amongst the crowd,
We prayed he'd smile behind the shroud,
We ached for him at any cost,
The lovely boy that we had lost.
Oh sure we knew this could not be,
He was only loaned to his dad and me,
But twenty years was not enough,
To carry on was mighty tough.
People prayed with all their might,
That God would send a spark of light
In our hour of darkness we were blind,
We yearned the peace we hoped to find.
Mary Mother she did know
The pain of having to let go.
The grief within, the sense of loss,
We had no choice but to bear our cross.
We forced ourselves and tried to pray,
Please Mary help us, we did say.
Send peace back home to our family,
Please take our son to Heaven with Thee.
There's many a miracle out in Lourdes,
Visible and invisible cures.
Mary helped us on our station,
She gave us peace and resignation.

Phil Robinson

MERCY

Justice is a human thing,
But mercy is divine
So when I look into this troubled heart of mine
I say be merciful to me O God
Be merciful this day
The trials of life are hard to bear
Our footsteps go astray
And yet he goes on giving, giving of His love.
He paints flower carpets for our feet
And hangs the stars above
Do we deserve these lovely things?
What have we done, that he
Should create for our delight
A thing as perfect as a tree
Just take a look around us
At the glories to be seen
The hills, the dales and meadows
With their forty shades of green
So I must give such love as this
To friend and enemy
Because the Great Creator
Has been merciful to me.

Bill Williamson

A CONSCIENCE PROBE

Can you help lift someone's burden,
Can you show you truly care,
Is your heart a peaceful garden,
When you're needed are you there?

Do you face your woes with courage,
Both your bread and feelings share,
Do you comfort or disparage,
Do you have some time to spare?

Are you tactful and forgiving
Or hold grudges, act through spite,
Do you know that life's for living,
Do you seek the wrongs to right?

Are you harmless and plain-speaking,
Take the risk to say what's true,
Are you caring or self seeking,
Do you start, then see it through?

Is your conscience clear and blameless,
Do you worship the Most High,
Are your dealings fair and gainless,
Do you strive, or fail to try?

Do you thank the world's Creator
For the gift of Life today,
Do you see His Will as greater,
Or just seek to have your way?

If your answers score with favour,
If you truly kindle love,
Then you give to life its flavour
And are blessed by Heaven above.

Emmanuel Petrakis

Hagar's Well

Exposed, rejected, wandering, lost,
I've come so far across hard land;
No shelter here, no helpful hand,
Now I can see no way ahead,
No power, no strength, not even bread.
From my child I turn my eyes,
I can no longer bear his cries,
I know I'm helpless as he dies.
Where is the God who sees?
Where is the God who cares?
I'm blind, for tears have filled my eyes.

A voice breaks in from far, yet near,
And whispers comfort in my ear,
Lifts my gaze, rebukes my fear;
'I am the God who sees;
I am the God who cares.'
The God, who knows him where he lies,
Says, 'I have heard the child's own cries.
Now see my well of water here,
Clear your eyes, as you draw near,
Find water fresh for you to fill
Your empty pot you carry still.
Now draw and fill it to the brim,
I will fulfil my plans for him.
So give it to the child with love,
As I am sheltering you above.
In deserts I will carry you,
And see your journey safely through;
For the sake of the child whose cry I hear,
Because I hold my children dear.'

Lydia Lyrics

NEW STRENGTH

From the depths of adversity
new strength shines so bright.
Deep within hearts, such hope and faith
forever see the light.

The history of yesterday
has passed and is gone.
Now go forward and be strong
soon the victory be won.

Many secrets learn about life
joys and pain both share.
Tomorrow's special mystery
raise sprits everywhere.

Every day believe in yourself
sun sparkles so true.
Silver linings amongst dark clouds,
today's a gift for you.

So journey to the rainbows end
promises fulfil.
Enrichment in fine treasures rare
tranquil skies, peace be still.

Margaret Jackson

LIGHT

When the light was nailed down
The skies began to close
But all they did was light the way
For future times to come.

When a loved one leaves your arms
And all around is dark
They'll always be beside us
If we listen with our hearts.

Hope and love eternal
In all embracing light
Life will spring from death
As day will grow from night.

John Holdsworth

Our New Tomorrow

Lift solemn hearts unto replenishing shore,
Conciliation abounds beyond distant stars,
Cast cynicism asunder thus caress no more,
Obeisance descend to conceal the scars,
Tomorrow convey compassion so refined.
Amid rapture seek solace to honour the same,
Upon paradise shall all share purity kind,
With angels' euphoria shall encumber our name.

Concur O tenderness upon freedom's trace,
Lest souls cower to perish amid obscurity,
Befall not to transgression before saving grace,
Hear O Redeemer vast laments of woe,
Amid disconsolate turbulence we faithful bow,
Upon our new tomorrow beyond stars to glow.
Sweet accolade caress souls weeping now,
Search horizons stretching in unison with dreams.

Heaven rejoice such everlasting morn,
Sing angels orchestral above valleys proud.
Thus fulfilment of sustenance stand newborn,
Upon mountains echo thy caressing shroud.
Be darkness cast, beyond sunshine's day.
Rainbow springs of crystal in delight
Portray obeisance and holiness upon the fray,
Our new tomorrow now eternally shine bright.

Steve Kettlewell

Remember Those

To you who only have one eye to see,
Remember those whose life in darkness be.
To you with one leg like a withered stalk,
Remember those who cannot even walk.
To you who only have one hand to touch,
Remember those who cannot hold a crutch.
To you that have a sound and healthy mind,
Remember those that nature left behind.
And those near perfect, yet think that life's not fair,
Get on your knees and thank God with a loving prayer.

Henry Brown Rowland

THANKS

The sunshine of your smile
Light
The stars in the sky
The shadows look tall

The moonbeam falls.
The rainbow peeks through
The silver cloud
That hides you
The bluebell smiles

Never cries.

Helen Owen

A CHURCH

A church has beauty, a church has history, a church has love,
A church is the place where you go, if you wish to talk to your
God up above.
A church is a place of welcome, for all who wish to be there,
The old, the sick and the lonely, may all have God's love to share.
The preacher will help the old people, in any way that he can,
He'll find company for the lonely, woman, child or man.
If you are sick or worried, the preacher will pray with you,
He'll help to strengthen your faith and belief, that God has
helped you through.
Once you've found the love of God, then thank him in every way,
By showing others what his love can do while living every day.
His church will become your second home, your friends and neighbours
will gather there,
To sing out some songs to their father above or to talk to him
in silent prayer.
So sing loud those hymns, and ring out those bells, way up in
the church steeple.
Let everyone know that God's love is in a church and it's given there
free to all people

Nita Garlinge

Let Your Spirit Fly

No one on earth could understand,
The pain I was going through,
But in my dreams a voice told me,
The answer lies inside of you.

No matter what life holds in store,
Your soul will still fly free.
Search your mind for memories,
And give your love to me.

Now when rain clouds hide the sun,
And my eyes just want to cry.
I think about my memories
And lift my spirit into the sky.

Try and hold on to the happy times,
Think about them every day,
And thank the Lord in Heaven
For showing you the way.

Remember when life fills with pain,
That no one else can see,
The Lord has given you memories,
To set your spirit free.

Lesley Allen

A Promise

One day there will be peace for all;
A promise has been made.
This broken world someday will fall,
And the Word of God be obeyed.

In mercy He waits till all have heard;
The whole world must be told
That God will never break His Word;
His promises will unfold.

Repent of past sins and truly believe,
Is all Jesus asks us to do.
The rest follows on - His love you receive,
And your faith He will daily renew.

God gave His Spirit, whose very breath
From doubts your mind will release,
And show you life need not end in death
But lead to eternal peace.

Joan Picton

When Your Mind Is Troubled

When your mind is troubled and feel no joy
Jesus will listen and he will reply
You are my child and I love you so
Do not worry I will be with you wherever you go
Do not be downhearted do not be sad
Just be grateful for the good times you've had
Everyone suffers their joys and their sorrows
Always hoping for a better tomorrow
Try to find a peace from within
Let Jesus's soul enter in
Just let him help you all he can
He is a treasured possession and a wonderful man.
When I look back through the years
He was there for me to share my sorrow and tears
So let us be grateful for him being there
Knowing at all times he will listen
To our prayer.

Glenis Dando

TAKE HEART

It's hard to come to terms with
We just don't understand
But take heart from the fact that Jesus
Was there to hold your loved one's hand.

Sometimes it's hard for us to imagine
The pain the bereaved ones are going through
But remember we're always here if you need us
And our prayers are always with you.

Please try not to feel so guilty
Although you're racked with pain
When God above decides its time
You'll meet in Heaven again.

Christina Carville

A Young Boy Walked These Streets

I taught my son to know the difference between right and wrong.
It seems to me you teach your boy that he should use a gun.
I watched you on the TV placing him right in harms way.
And caught up in the cross-fire, I saw your son die today.
I won't forget the image of the fear upon his face.
An innocent young victim killed in such a Holy place.
I know you feel your cause is just, but it appears to me.
That what it is you're seeking, could be achieved peacefully.
I can't pretend to understand how tough life's been for you.
I try to think how I'd react, if I were in your shoes.
I know it's hard, but you should learn to forgive if you can.
So that your neighbour's child might do the same when he's a man.
It's written - let he without sin be first to cast the stone.
Please try to teach your young men they should leave those rocks alone.
I wonder if God's watching, or has he now washed his hands?
As he witnesses *his* children defiling the Holy Land.
In the midst of battle, I watch both sides stop to pray.
Then you carry on the killing, which just fills me with dismay.
Tomorrow when you bury your son, don't let it be in vain.
His death will count for nothing, if the hatred still remains.
Long ago a young boy walked these streets where you now fight.
You owe it to his memory to try to put things right.
There's many contradictions, but the worst I ever saw
Is when you call this carnage in Israel - a Holy War!

Roger A Carpenter

LOVE WHERE HAVE YOU GONE?

Love, love where have you gone?
Why is the world doing so much wrong?
Where is the melodious music so sweet?
Love songs that made your heart miss a beat,
Where are the couples whispering, 'I love you?'
With a beautiful wedding day in view.
Where are the churches filled to the door,
With people singing God's praises for evermore?
Where are the happy families around the fire,
And laughter filling every heart's desire?
Where is the glorious sun up on high,
The moon and the stars that light the night sky?
It seems that darkness has taken their place,
Where it once was a happy, delightful place.
God's world is now filled with misery,
Oh when will He come to set us free?
God, when will your love return to us once more?
When all know that it's you we should adore!
Joy will only come back when we all unite,
And radiate your world with glorious light.

Nicky Young

BLINDING LIGHT

Tumbling down a spiral of light
Earth-bound yet floating through the sky
Lightning bolts like snow whirling, cold to my face yet warm
Restless as in a dreamland but awake
Like a nutritionist pondering a diet
Or an Irishman talking to the Blarney Stone
Could this be a dream, a moment of woe
Or perhaps a prayer on the rebound
'Ah!' Now there lies a second once foretold
Heaven and Earth unite through the universe like a cord
Invisible to see yet heartfelt for me
Passing from conscious to subconscious
I feel a presence within my heart
Yet it was always there! Like a little gold star awaiting birth
Could prayer be so powerful, so overpowering
Yet tranquil and bliss, levitating and restful

Douglas Bonthron

Loving Service

Give a helping hand
Lend a listening ear
Show a grieving brother
That you really care.

Lose yourself for others
Fill a human need
Show you are a Christian
Not only in word but deed

Lighten the load of another
Go that extra mile
Give a weary traveller
A warm and kindly smile.

Love is like a boomerang
It always comes back to you
The more you give, the more you get
Seems strange, but it's very true.

Genevieve Tuke

FIGHT THE FIGHT

I look through the window
And see a battle of dark and light,
The archangels from Heaven and the demons from below,
Locked in conflict over who should claim my lost soul.

For I had stepped back into the darkness you see,
To seek out the shadows and devour the seed of evil
that was living in me.
I did not understand then, that I could not destroy what was
part of myself,
To try only fuels the fires of anger and hate,
Giving the demons tighter hold over my dwindling fate.

Now I realise I must embrace it to be whole,
To accept that it is part of me, might well be what saves my soul.
As now the hate and anger's gone, replaced by love
and understanding,
The battle is over
The demons are gone
Only Angels remain standing.

Sally Bush

In The Hands Of God

We walk in the hands of God,
even the sad times mean something to Him,
and when we lie under the sod,
our souls will go back where it is not grim.

We walk in the hands of God
and so we bless His name,
in dark times onward we must plod,
because with Him it will not be the same.

We walk in the hands of God,
and if there is no fame,
life for our back has made a rod,
in this there is no shame.

We walk in the hands of God,
His mercy will combine,
the labourer with his hod,
and folks who think they're fine.

We walk in the hands of God,
He knows what we will do,
when He could walk through lod,
the people knew it too.

Jean Paisley

A Prayer Answered

God helped me in my hour of need
when my prayer He answered.
My son had died
and was being laid to rest.
So I was feeling 'flustered'
as I walked out from my front door,
(without pre-meditation).
I looked up to the sky and begged,
'Please God help me endure
the pain of loss, this day,
and help me understand,
why you had to take him
to Your heavenly land.'
I went to church, joined in the hymns,
I knew I must be brave,
I watched sadly as they laid him
in his long, low grave.
God gave me the strength and courage
to take this bitter blow.
He dried my eyes, tho' sometimes now
secret tears still flow.
So, if someone has a problem
and no one seems to care,
tell your troubles to God above
for He listens to every prayer.

May Dabrowiecki

To Harry

Can't believe I've joined the gang
Of heads bowed low and eyes on ground.
Pushing a trolley is new to me.
'I'll never do that' I'd always found.

You think that things will never change
As day by day you live your life
Doing things automatically
You think you'll always be a wife.

But life is full of dirty tricks
Just when you think things are okay.
The bubble bursts, hits you for six
The ground below is swept away.

I did not think I'd ever lose
The rock you were beneath my feet
Always there to welcome me
When I came home, sometimes dead beat.

The silence is unbearable
No one to answer when I speak
The problems now unsolvable
No one to give advice I seek.

You think you can't go on this way
Wrapped in your cloak of selfishness
But look around as every day
Others are also in this mess

Sybil Chard

DEAR GOD

Dear God

Thank you for your gift, my life,
Thank you for my health,
Thank you for my happiness,
My security, independence and love.
Thank you for my sight
Thank you for everything,
For listening and showing you care,
Most of all thank you for always being there.

Danielle Gallagher

A Dedication To Husband Sid

There is a cherry tree that stands.
It blooms so freely on grassy land
It constantly reminds me of our precious love
A love that was shared and memories of
The cherry tree is like a symbol of faith
Letting me know that you are safe.

Dorothy Bender

NOW YOU ARE GONE

The wind was caressing my cheek
As I stood and looked at the view.
It seemed to know I needed help
To ease the pain of losing you.

Where have you gone my beloved?
I miss you, oh so much.
I miss the sound of your voice;
I still miss your tender touch.

You gave me so much that was good,
It was a joy to live each day.
I never gave thought to the fact
That I might lose you this way.

We had so many years of love
Still to live together, I'm sure.
Now I grieve and cry and wonder why
We weren't even able to say goodbye.

Hazel Devonshire

TRUST

Lord, I had a problem
At the close of day,
It was overwhelming
As I knelt to pray.

When I should be praising
Thanking you for all;
Worry held me captive
In a world so small.

Through the hours of darkness
Reaching out to you,
Caring. Loving Father
Show me what to do.

Then as dawn was breaking
Chasing off the night;
Still my soul was seeking
Comfort from the light.

While the sun is rising
Radiant in the sky,
Send your Holy Spirit
All my needs supply.

As the day grew stronger
So was I restored,
Loved, upheld, supported
Praise to you my Lord

E Anderson

MEDITATION

How can I begin to say
How wisdom leads me on my way
It's both a feeling and a word
Which springs into my silent world
If I relax my self away -
My needs and fears and urge to pray
Instead just listen in humility
To that warm space in you and me
Which links the world in unity
Eternal positive energy
Wraps its way around my mind
Expands my consciousness to find
Understanding of my faults and sins
And in so doing, compassion springs
For all of us in the human race
Who play our parts, project a face
When underneath in our inner world
Our true self waits to finally evolve
- Into that spiritual being
We forgot we were
When we were
Born.

Brenda Dove

BLESSINGS

The storm has passed.
The sky shines clear blue,
Alive with the swoop and cry of swallows.
Lazy in the garden stands the plum tree
Its branches bent with fruit
Rich red and touched by the sun.
Tomorrow they will be ready,
When the cool mist ebbs, and
The sun has dried them.
We will climb the ladder and
Laughing pick them all - all we can reach
And boil them dangerously as
The sweet steam rises.
In jars they will sit,
Shining like the summer sun,
Glowing clear and ruby red.
One by one the jars will be eaten
As the days shorten, and
Darkness draws near.
We will remember the laughter,
And the swoop of swallows.

A L Skevington

THANK YOU GOD
FOR ORDINARY PEOPLE

I just don't know
what's happened
here this week,
So much love
So much compassion;
So much worry!

Thank you God

For ordinary men
Average men
You know what
I mean!
They're not
pretending to be
Something they're not,
They shouldn't do
They don't need to.

Just ordinary blokes,
Ordinary.

With ordinary relationships
Ordinary marriages
(or divorces!)
Ordinary feelings;
Ordinary emotions.

In ordinary jobs
Just bus drivers,
Ordinary 'man-talk'
Ordinary men.

Thank you God
For ordinary people.

People that I love
With everything
I am made of.

Josephine Reading

A LETTER TO GOD

If I could write to God, what words would I say?
Something like, 'Thank you, for this hour and day,'
Then I would write, and to him I'd tell,
'I am so lucky thank you Lord, I am feeling well,'
It's not God I'd blame, for my silly spill,
I would not blame him when children die
I would not blame God, for earthquakes severe,
I would thank him, yes, for my good cheer,
How often I've wondered, 'What would I say,
And how much would it cost,
To post all that way?'

V V Oliver

My Battle Won

First I panicked, teary eyed,
Thought up excuses and little white lies.
So I wouldn't feel stupid
And have to pretend,
That it was a bad dream,
I would wake up in the end.

Next I felt sick, so unfair,
Why should you be there and how could you dare?
To make me feel stupid,
And have to go through,
Yet another nightmare day,
With the nightmare being you.

Then I felt strong, determined,
To face this last battle, fight you and win.
So I wouldn't feel stupid,
Again question 'How?'
For I can now see its purpose,
And I've won my battle now.

I've accepted, yesterday,
As fate's turned its tide and now you will pay.
I will no more feel stupid,
I can now move on,
The nightmare's gone forever,
Through the fight, I turned out strong.

Kate Stobart

MORE THAN GOLD

He looked for the end of the rainbow in vain
After clasping his hands in despair and in pain,
There was no silver lining to temper the cloud,
He was down on his knees, he was battered and bowed.

Then a stranger who'd travelled the same road before
Said 'If any man enter, for I am the Door,
You are clasping your hands, you are down on your knees,
Come now, close your eyes, God will answer your pleas.'

Peter Davies

OUR FATHER

Only, when times are hard,
Do we cry out in our despair,
Uttering the words, once taught,
To one of whom, we are unaware.
Reliving childhood practices,
We place our trust, in God.
Father, help us, we do cry,
When things go amiss.

Aimlessly we wander, through this veil of tears,
Trusting in our own prowess,
To take us through the years.
Help we often need, but know not where to turn.
Evil often claims us, without us being aware.
Take thought for what may happen, do not despair.
Remember He who created, each and every one,
Ask the Father for his help,
Make God, your number one.

Jane Dyson

Pipe Dream

I live amidst a hurricane,
a cyclone of selfish hate.
Some just cannot stand the thought of peace,
only supremacy will sate.

I absorb sobs of ancient pain,
silent centuries of death;
can millennium the killing cease,
or is that hope a waste of breath?

I am Ireland, my soul is strained
with the blood of innocents.
Millennium is no Golden Fleece,
children; live for the present tense!

Perry McDaid

STRIVE FOR CONTENTMENT

It's hard to comprehend the reasons
We experience troubled seasons
Nature is bound to see climates through
Each one of us must brave winter too
In weaving our soul's rich tapestry
Dark and threads are necessary
Understanding, as time unravels,
That we gain wisdom from our travels
Arrows which pierce us we must endure
Why pain? What gain? We hope to mature
All sent to crack our ignorant shield
Freeing wisdom to be next revealed
It is unwise too much to ponder
Knowing all - where would be earth's wonder!
What a dull, boring place it would be
Gone would be the thrill of mystery
Worthwhile striving for at any cost
Before the opportunity's lost
Is faith so strong it does not waver
When times don't appear in our favour
Make contentment the name of the game
Lesser wants resting save this main aim
Then even when troubles do draw near
Inner peace will protect you from fear.

Tina Lipman

DISTURBING THE BALANCE

Spring flew by so very fast,
I thought the summer had come at last,
But it brought the rain, wind and autumn blast,
Cold, cold days and frosty nights,
How chill the wind, into flesh it bites.

Buddleia, honeysuckle, the roses bough,
Chill winds and rains have dashed them now,
Cold dark days, a cloudy sky,
Bushes and flowers in bloom, once more they try.

What has become of those halcyon days?
Who's disturbed the balance and changed nature's ways?

Man!

June Ann Prescott

THE LIGHT OF JESUS

Oh Lord Jesus please show us the light
Shield us from the darkness of night
Show us all the good things we've had
Then we'll know life's not so bad

Those who are lonely, spend hours alone
No physical contact, just mobile phone
To shake someone's hand or give them a cuddle
Or will the mind remain in a muddle?

So Lord Jesus I don't mean to be rude
Lots can be done with your spiritual food
Release us from the gloom and doom
Bring your light to my darkest room

Give me strength to project that light
To someone else with a similar plight
And raise a smile on numerous faces
Introduce them to the social graces

And those who are at the end of their tether
Renew their faith as we pray together
Now dear Lord please show them you care
Bring light to their world of fear and despair.

Stanley Swann

A HELPING HAND

I'll hold your hand through thick and thin
To keep you strong when trouble begins
The strength will flow from me to you
Joined together we'll all pull through
When the cloud has passed on by
We'll use our hands to wave it goodbye.

If we need help we just need to say
Someone is there to ease it away
A trouble shared with a comforting friend
Is always much smaller in the end
Don't be afraid to help out too
Others have troubles just like you.

By caring and sharing and helping each other
You're sure to feel better one way or another.

Marion Pollitt

Ripples

A single pebble,
In a still pond,
Makes *ripples* that echo to the edge.

A single word,
In a small group,
Affects each one
Like *ripples,* and echoes on forever.

A single act,
Might help just one
But it will carry on like *ripples,*
And echo on forever.

A single person,
Can change many lives,
With words and acts and prayers.
The *ripples* will echo on forever.

We make many *ripples* and sometimes *waves.*
Our words and acts and prayers,
Inspire many, and touch their lives,
And the *ripples* echo on forever.

Rosemary Taylor

VOICE OF HOPE

Enter into a silent house
To sit in dapple shade
To think - talk and ask why
We ask for help - to see us through
We tell of joys - laughter - fears - sorrow
And the worries of tomorrow
Problems great and small we've shared
He listens and guides us when we're scared
Though I sit alone, in thought
I was not alone, he taught us how
To hear - the still small voice of calm.

David Charles

DADDY . . .

The day you left I cried all day
It seemed as though there was no other way
The father I had loved for twenty-one years
Comforted me when I was unhappy, but now
Couldn't wipe away these tears.

I couldn't bear the shock or the pain
I wanted to do something, find someone to blame
For taking away my father who gave me so much love
But it was His decision, the almighty one above.

A week has now passed, yet today I felt so alone
As I walked away from the cemetery and my father's stone
The sadness of your loss began to fill my eyes
As I prayed for you then finally, said my goodbyes.

I know that you will be with me in all that I do
Yet I fear for the future, having to face it without you
To have my father back would be my only wish
Yet God has given me your memories to love and cherish.

The times we had spent were so valuable together
The memories of us as a family will stay with me forever
Yet every day I am left to face that one empty seat
Daddy . . . My life without you will forever be incomplete.

Farah Gilani

REFLECTION

Like a leaf, in the breeze
On the air, in its ease
But it can't, in itself
Make a change

Like a candle, burning bright
In the darkness, of the night
Short lived, so it can't
Make a change

Like a cloud, in the sky
Drifting along, way up high
I know, that it won't
Make a change

Like myself, just a man
I've tried, all I can
And even I, don't
Make a change

However . . .

If that leaf, in the breeze
Inspires, a poet's ease
Then it has, in effect
Made a change

If that candle, burning bright
Gives the poet, the vision to write
Then it has, without doubt
Made a change

If that cloud, in the sky
Forms the rain, from way on high
That feeds the drought, it has
Made a change

Therefore I, a lonely man
Can strive to do, all I can
So that I, in my way
Can also make a change.

Kevin Murphy

HEAR US FATHER

Heavenly Father hear us when we softly call Your name.
We have only You to help us when our lives are filled with pain.
It may be pain of illness, or relationships gone sour,
But Lord You are our mainstay in our lonely hour.
We humbly beseech You to hold us in Yours arms
And as we feel the comfort, we too can strew our palms
Of thankfulness and happiness as You give us back our health,
And we come to realise we have enormous wealth,
In all the care You give us and the daily bread we share.
It's only right and proper that we give You thanks in prayer,
So Holy Heavenly Father as we kneel before Your throne,
We ask that You will take our lives and lead us gently home.

Jennie Schofield

In These Troubled Times (Israel)

In troubled times
when bullets fire,
in twisted smoky haze.
Above blue skies,
With floods of sunlight,
while my ears break to the sound
of the thumping of my heart.
Blood gathers in each solitary drip,
to form a vein of thin red,
flowing into twisted capillaries,
The end of a family tree.
Can we speak of freedom,
with the firing of a gun.

Paul Darby

EYE HATH NOT SEEN

Eye never has seen, nor indeed has the ear heard,
Neither has man's heart conceived, the glories to be shared
In those lofty mansions the Saviour has gone to prepare,
For, when we awake in His likeness, what wonders we'll find there.

Through heaven's immense jasper walls and open pearly gates,
And from its jewelled foundation, there powerfully radiates
The full spectrum of colours, dazzling, bright and gleaming,
With the most brilliant light, through the heavenly city streaming.

And inside the pearly gates, further marvels we'll behold -
The tree and river of life, and the streets of pure gold;
Then that soul-thrilling moment, when, united with God's Son,
We at last see His face, the Altogether Lovely One.

And, midst indescribable beauties, there'll be no more crying,
For pain has been vanquished, as have sadness and dying,
Where all the ransomed shall join on that great homecoming day,
With songs, joy and gladness, as sighing and sorrow flee away.

And we'll be abundantly satisfied with heaven's rich treasures,
As God makes us drink of the rivers of His pleasures,
For, at His right hand we shall find such for evermore,
And Christ bids us to enter, because He is the Door.

For He arose from the dead, yes, Hallelujah, He lives,
And to all who trust Him as Saviour a living hope He gives -
An inheritance reserved in the land of endless day,
Undefiled, incorruptible, to never fade away.

So take heart, dear soul, though vexed with cares here below,
And rejoice at the prospect one glorious day you will know -
For our present light affliction, 'tis but temporary,
And brings a far more exceeding, eternal weight of glory.

Ian Caughey

LIGHT AND SHADE

It's odd to contemplate the role
of chance that scuppers dreams and plans
Our politicians laid on line
In glossy manifesto's claims
Before election's ballyhoo.
Complexity ensures the fall
Of pundits who declare the route
Of future's train. The roll of dice
Derails deterministic rules.
It's thus we find the need for choice
Between the unpredicted forks
That show our maps are out of date.
While free to join the mob in wild
Stampede of startled swine, we choose
To stand our ground to contemplate
A better way. Beneath the noise
Of warring thoughts a silent voice,
That's Word of love divine, is heard
By those who crave to do what's right.
They may not know that inner goad
Is gift of God, but never mind
As long as prod evokes response
That's steeped in a deceitless love
For world of light and shade, without
Resort to force or fear. We search,
We strive, we take the knocks. We spurn
The calls of those who seek revenge.
We place our trust in path of hope.

Henry Disney

Faith And Rejection

For some the song it sounded sweet
For others could not hear it
For some the vision they could see
Others could not see it
For some live by the truth alone
Others only use it
For some his words are rich and strong
But others could not read it
For some have faith
And others don't think they need it.

Maxwell Anderson

Until Jesus Comforted Me

Head on my pillow filled with sorrow,
Nothing left to see,
Another day, another tomorrow
Until Jesus comforted me.

A shattered heart to be mended,
One more unanswered plea,
Another lonely day has ended
Until Jesus comforted me.

My days were filled with pain,
No longer could I feel free,
All the years would seem the same
Until Jesus comforted me.

Frank Parker

Changed But Unchanging

At first love was unchanging,
A tactile mapping of another being,
Likes and dislikes,
As it grew it surrounded others,
Welcomed them within.
Mature love rode the waves of life,
Faced the gremlins and the gifts.
Illness brought a subtle change of role,
Providing little services with humour,
Trying not to demean.
But now love faces the severest test,
As the Ruler starts to draw the line.
Love must learn unselfishness,
Relinquish the ties so long binding,
In love to await,
The Reunion.

Di Bagshawe

For You

I want to send a healing ray
Of love, of joy to you,
Pour balm upon the hurts that bind,
And calm the storms that brew.

I want to breathe out clear air
And whisk away the pain
That's carried heavy on your heart,
This suff'ring has no gain.

I want to feed your soul with light
To wash away the dark,
And lift you up, up to the heights,
Away from all that's stark.

I want to help you through all this,
And yet, I don't know how.
I throw my arms around your pain,
And trust you'll pull through now.

By myself I'm nothing,
And there's nothing I can do
But send you love through my heart,
The love that's loving you.

I want to say some lovely words,
My tongue is stuck like glue.
Although the sounds just cannot flow
I write this just for you.

Judith Thomas

In Troubled Times

On the death of a friend.

The long slow stumble
Towards the end of a life
Hurts like nettles
On a bruised waiting soul.

Movements falter and fumble.
The mind hesitates
And precious petals
Of irreplaceable seconds unfold.

A shared memory; a joke;
A conversation murmured in a quiet corner;
A last meal; a drink; choked
Emotions suppressed in a novice mourner.

A silence that holds vital secrets firm.
Shared questions lie unanswered - mute -
Clouds gather as you squirm
With feelings of neglect, hopelessness, fear and guilt.

Your lifetime friend:
The shared soul of your being
Fades and pales towards their final scene
Soothing you with thoughts of support.

Have faith:
Life's only a momentary dream.

R J Westwell

Lift Me Up

Reach out to me, for I am lost.
Wandering in a wilderness.
Where I am, is barren.
Nothing here that points the way.
Desolate is this place, so cold, so grey.
Lift me up! Help me away!
I can't stay here another day.

Raymond K Evans

All Saints And The Pilgrim Fathers

Let me tell you a tale about a church at Babworth
And a group of people called the Pilgrim Fathers
Who wanted to worship in freedom
But somehow rose to fame.

Lead by their vicar of All Saints
Like thieves they sneaked out in round
The back in the night
Men, women and children
They had to do what they thought right.

Turning their backs on their homes
They headed for the Coste
They boarded a ship bound for Holland
With hope shining out of their eyes.

However Holland was not for them
So they sailed to a place called
Massachusetts Bay
That place is known as America
And the ship was called The Mayflower.

I'm very proud to live in Retford
Babworth Church
Is just over the bridge
I sometimes walk the way
Of the Pilgrim Fathers
It always reminds me of what they did.

Freda Lily Lawrence

Thank You

Thank you dear Lord,
For not needing to fight with a sword.
Thank you for being there,
For taking the time to care
Over the problems I have had to face.
Thank you for your love and grace.
My battles have been won,
Through the dying of your son.
Never again do I have to live in fear,
As I feel your love and know you're near.

Elizabeth Jones

All The World's Sorrow

Splash of a tear on smooth high rock
vanishes in the sand.
Over rougher rock a tear lingers
slips, rolls adrift
leaving a salty trace.
Dripping in the hollowed rock
tear on tear hits, insists
lays bare the nerve ends of the earth.
Relentless patient tears for millions of years
wept or kept
now hounding pounding wash the grit away
touch the rock-heart must be broken
bent, melted, fused
transformed at last
as Jesus dies on the cross.

The font brims over:
Of rejections, of banishment, of losses
of rapes, of wars, of genocide,
of mournings.

Beasts, birds and
humans
drink the sorrow away.

Françoise de Pierpont

Wandering Child

It is when we find ourselves
at that very darkest time of life.
When everything we try to do,
seems to turn against us -
and every new road we travel,
leads to another dead end.
When it seems our prayers
all go unanswered.

This is the very moment -
when the clouds will part.
A voice will speak,
through the mind of man -

'My wandering child,
did you really think I had forsaken you?
The roads you had chosen to follow,
would have taken you into bitter despair.
It was I, who gently guided you back.

I am the light -
in your darkest hour.
I shine, for all eternity.'

Nina Graham

JOSEPH

Mary was told by the spirit to be
silent to Joseph concerning the
Annunciation.
That he would be informed in due course.
Mary, who had visited Elizabeth
And remained until the birth of John
Was met by Joseph, her condition
Apparent . . . tormenting Joseph,
By what source?
Mary speaks little, Joseph's pain showing
For three days they suffered
A terrible passion.
As Mary sits in the shade of an apple tree
Patiently spinning, Joseph comes,
He says 'I want you to forgive me,
Why have you been so humble as to
Conceal your *glory.'*
She said in a whisper 'If I had not
I would not deserve to conceive
The unexpected One.'
Their tears fall on a rarely revealed story.

Anne Seymour

Title Conflict

Images flicker people lay dying
Orphaned, the children lost crying
Distracted, unseeing I turn away
To watch my children free at play
Laughter echoes from the garden swing
Cloudscaped sky, fledglings on the wing
Below are clusters of golden flowers
Awakened by the soft spring showers
Relentless the television drones on
Bewildered, sobbing, refugees, another bomb.

I watch remote at so much pain
The maimed and dying, have I no shame
I press the switch and blank the screen
Will I forget what I have seen?
My children call, a bird lies dying
Now they are sad, both are crying
In a small white box we lay to rest
The fledgling that fell from its nest
And I vow to send a large donation
But will it heal a divided nation?

Sheila Pharo

RESPECT

The Flander's fields are again red,
Where our soldiers once did tread.
Years ago many lost their life,
Remembered by pals who did survive.

Many still have time to remember,
We carry poppies - the 11th of November.
In silence we bow our heads to pray,
For all the people who died far away.

The poppies are a sign of respect,
For all the men, some never met.
For the families of the last war,
Some lonely, and some are poor.

People now pray hard for peace,
Hoping all wars will soon cease.
Let the poppy of remembrance grow,
In a true world we love to know.

We respect what we know is right,
And we don't want to have to fight.
We only want the poppies to show,
Our respect for the people, friend or foe.

Margaret Upson

A Widow's Prayer

As I kneel to wash my kitchen floor
I say a prayer, and ask God for
Strength and energy for my work and play,
With His love to guide me through each day.
That in this darkness He will hold my hand,
And my grief He will understand.
As I look towards that empty chair
For the one I loved who's no longer there.
Because it's not easy these tasks to do
When you know there is no one coming home to you.
To say 'Hello love, what's for tea?
How's your day been? Did you miss me?'
But I will try, for as life must go on,
The wound God is healing, as He helps me along.
My broken heart in time He will mend,
As with each new day I pray He will send,
New friends, new ventures for me to try -
When sorrow comes suddenly, you need to ask 'Why?'
As often I'm lonely, sometimes I'm sad,
But I count my blessings for the love that I had.
All the sweet memories of the way that He cared,
Of our years together, and all that we shared.

Eileen Wood

THANKS BE

Blind was I, now I see
Sickness of soul, now well.
Belief in God's love for me
'His' wondrous miracles to tell.

When in sorrow
Doubt of self
Each morrow
Prayer will help

Gazing at beauty all around
Meadows lush, fields, hills
Listening to music, bird sounds
My heart with pleasure fills.

Thanking God for creation
Beauty of earth
With joy, elation
Ever praise Him in my church.

Ivy Lott

MOMENTS

The birth of my daughter
You gave to me
So warm and precious
With love divine
And it breaks my heart
It's so unkind
Please God, don't take her from me
The pain will last for Eternity
So please dear God
Keep her life on hold
And take me first as I am old.

Please don't deal me life, in a cruel way
Because she needs to stay
Don't take her from me
As I would die inside
As I bless the day you gave her to me
Her children's eyes would be full of tears
Every moment, every day
I pray to you God, to let her stay.

Inside I cannot bear the pain
So I beg and pray, when I talk to thee
The children she bore with love and joy
The pain they will feel will break my heart
So take me instead, and give her life
You can't take her, she belongs to me
So please clear Lord, come down to earth
And hold her tight with love divine
And please protect a daughter - of mine

Ann Marie Stokes

Jesus,
Greatest Of All Heroes

His arm is mightier than Jove's
To make mountains move.

His shoulders are broader than Atlas's
To carry the whole world safely.

His eye is keener than Apollo's
To see into men's souls.

With greater compassion than conceited Narcissus
He surveys the muddy image of mankind.

His beauty eclipses handsome Adonis's
To brighten darkened lands.

Venus's glittering star sets upon a cold gravestone
But His love shines all night through.

When His path leads across the sea
His feet merrily dance upon the deep.

If towering waves should begin to swell and crest
Then with soothing verse, He stills Neptune's troubled breast.

As slothful Pan sleeps from drinking too much alcohol
He the good shepherd, hears the lost lamb's bleating call.

But Jesus' new wine washes away man's sins
And is sweeter and redder than any that Bacchus drinks.

Yet how He cried like a helpless baby
Before He carried His cross to Calvary.

But with more strength than Samson could draw
From his locks of long hair
Jesus broke His chains of death on Easter Sunday
And flew above the clouds into the sky
Higher than Icarus ever dared
And brighter than any star.

Sean O'Brien

Now Is The Time (For The Healing Of Wounds)

Now is the time to heal the wounds
That have festered long
In their secret tombs
Now is the time
It is time now -
The wounds have been wound up
And ground down

Apply the poultice of soothing balm
Then, rub in the salt
And feel its sting
Shatter the heart of calm!

I am that walking wounded one -
You never miss
Your love attacks me everywhere
And my life-blood has spilt
From every wound
You ever thought you mended
With a kiss.

But only I can heal them now -
One by one
I close each painful tear
And so will boldly bear
The scars that will remain.

For it is our scars,
Born from such deep sorrow
And such pain,
That show us deeply
What we truly are.

Jane Phillimore

Show Me Your Glory

Dear Lord, I am weary of monotonous travel.
Here I am in the valley of Horeb mountain,
Even my shoes are full of sand and gravel.
Yet, I have an audience with the living fountain!
I have contentious questions to ask
Concerning your word. The promises you give.
Leading these people is an awesome task.
I only want to know, will we at least live?
You keep telling me in your sight I've found grace,
That you even know my Hebrew name.
We have talked face to face
But I long to see you all the same.
I hear your voice in a hiding cloud
But where are you?
It is not enough; am I allowed
To beg for a clearer view?
You tell me I have your heart
And I do your will
But this arduous valley experience tears me apart,
To see your presence, peace be still!
In the cleft of the rock, hidden by your Son
You passed by me
Not seen by everyone,
Your backward parts I did see.
Oh I see for sure that you are very close.
Only now can I endure
Any valley, through the power of the Holy Ghost.

Lloyd Noyes

FREETOWN

There is a place I love
Yet my mind could not be
Toward these people
Should I cast them out of my sight
They ask me, shall we go forth
What shall I tell them
Such as are for death, to death
And such as are for the sword, to the sword
The sword to slay and
The dogs to tear
And the beasts of the earth
To devour and destroy
Who will bereave them of children
Since they return not from their ways
Her sun is gone down
While it was yet day
What is our iniquity
What is our sin
Peace is taken away from this people
Even loving kindness and mercies.

Ebenezer Essuman

Jesus Is Near

There are times when life looks too tough,
The road ahead is going to be rough,
But 'Do not fear!' the Bible says,
Jesus, your Saviour, is always near.
When you're happy, joyful or sad,
Whether tearful, jolly or mad,
'Do not fear!' the Bible says
'Jesus, your Saviour, is always near.'

When trouble comes along your way,
Look to the Lord and these words say,
'Lift me now and give me grace,
For Jesus died in my place.'
It matters not what you've done,
Whether you've lost or whether you've won.
We do not have to win every race,
For Jesus died in *my* place.

Julie D Coventry

BREAKTHROUGH

It's in the little things
That love sends out its warming rays.
In the dark-soft gleam
Of a rising dawn
Tinting the pale-pink petals to a magentian glow
Streaming light
Creeping across the dank-dark shadows of the night
Disperses the shades of gloom
'Til the glory of the golden sun
Bursts through the portals of the bonded soul
And loosening the bands
Raises the hearts and mind
Beyond the finite
To the touch of the Creator's hands
And the promise of life incarnate.

Beryl Johnson

WITH JESUS

Tell me where are those creatures of light
Now passed away and gone from our sight?
They're seeing things our eyes have not seen
They are in places where we have not been.
They walk with Jesus in endless day
They praise the Saviour for ever and aye.
Sorrows and sufferings, sickness and pain
They do not have and will not have again.
Theirs the delights of which we are told;
Theirs is the face of the Lord to behold.
Worship, communion and praise without end
Spending each moment with our dearest friend.
Though we may miss them, now they're not here,
Our is the blessing of memories dear
Leave them to rest in that heaven of rest
Until the glad day when we too, shall be blessed.

Catherine May

MIRAGE 2000

I had a vision, within my sleep,
Where men did pray, and women weep,
A hot dry wind did fill the air,
As the vast multitude did stand and stare,
At the man nailed to the cross of wood
Between two thieves, one bad and good,
The man on the cross, he wept in pain,
As he died for mankind, yet it would all be in vain.

John J Hudson

The Trap

Troubled times are always with us
If we feel the need for plenty;
People's lives are most efficient
When they own what is sufficient.
It all starts when parents give us
All the toys that we would cry for,
Stamp our feet and sulk and sigh for;
We leave home, feel unrewarded;
We don't ask 'Can I afford it?'
Land in debt and things get sordid.
Poor folk suffering oil the wheels
Of our trade, big business steals
Sweet contentment with its greed
Pushing things we do not need.
When we finally expire
We won't go to Hells of fire
Get a message from the Lord
In Heaven no earthly goods are stored.
We'll arrange to send you back
You can't buy the joy you lack!

Leo Taylor

HOME AT LAST

I feel at peace, home at last,
now I can see my future and
forget the past.

With you to guide me I fear no one
I will not rest until my work is done.
I will give to people the will to live,
then come to you and
myself I give.

Sue Cox

A Refugee's Trinity

I heard the peace!
The guns at rest!
The birds all singing like angels blessed.
Then I awoke from my dream
by the sound of a cry, a howling scream.
Our home a wreck, our valuables gone!
But dear Lord in you, we've learnt to carry on!
Then amidst the settling dust,
a broken picture! An old hard crust!
Golden sunshine lit our window bright,
and we knew we would sleep safe
in our own beds this night!

O holy spirit encircling down,
like rays of bright sunlight
from God's Heavenly crown!
Send us your blessings, surround us with your love,
rebuild lives broken who's faith was unceased.
As we look for your glory! And a world built on peace!
A world united as in the three in One!

James Ellis

When Trouble Comes

When trouble comes
And you need care,
Talk to God,
Just say a prayer.

Reach out to Him,
Let Him take your hand.
Ask him to evidently
Help show you around.

The more time spent with Him,
The more comfort and care.
Whatever your trouble,
Take it to God in prayer.

Julie Sennitt

THERE AT HEAVEN'S DOOR

You know your family's
There for you
In times of tears and stress
They comfort, give you strength
And guide to quiet happiness
As time begins to heal once more
You look back to the days
When life was wonderful and new
So-called our younger days
The memories you have are precious
All that's gone before
Until one day you reach
Your loved one
There at Heaven's door

Jeanette Gaffney

A Presence

A presence comes into my room
It's there although unseen,
It's there up on the cornice
And enters through my dream.

The sun shines thro' the windowpane
Making stars upon the brass,
And there the presence is again
A star to shine, and then to pass.

A presence by the garage door
With the birds as they fly by,
It comes again, then disappears
With a smile from way up high.

Phyllis Ludgate

A Plea To God

Oh, all-knowing power that covers the world,
Be with us, have unbiased kindness.
For Thou art the last resort, when we are hurled
Against luck, to give body and mind rest.

With feeble mind and sickly soul
We're ruled by our fickle emotions.
God give us that we may once more unfold
And rise up from all base notions.

Our minds may drift-like the summer's rain
Through life's declines and promotions -
god give that we rise and breathe again
Unvanquished by life's corrosions.

Though we should fail Thee now and then
Chide us not too severely,
For though we betray Thee time and again,
At heart we love Thee sincerely.

Though we should cast Thee now and then
Chide us not too severely,
For though we betray Thee time and again,
At heart we love Thee sincerely.

Though we should cast Thee off in our pride
And haughtily strut independent,
Remember we know, though we boastingly stride,
At heart, that we're always dependent

Though we might swear that we need Thee not
And gaily disown and deny Thee,
Remember, we know when life threatens to clot,
That we crumple and haste to be nigh Thee.

Nina Havers

THE LORD IS MY SHEPHERD . . .

Are you there, dear Lord,
In the deep, deepest night,
When morbid thoughts prevail?
Can you hear me, Lord,
When I call on you for guidance
And destructive worries assail?
    Can I turn to you
    In my darkest hour,
    Will you help
    In my travail?

I had called out to you,
When I had no other help, you see,
I had listened, and heard your voice,
'My child, take heart, and hear *me,*
In my solemn words, rejoice,
For I am here, ever at your side,
When you thought you were so alone,
Please let me, always, be your guide,
Do not attempt life's journey, on your own.'

He will help you, as He has helped me,
Only place your trust in Him,
And He will carry your burden, effortlessly,
Near or far, wherever you are,
Through the sadness of life, let Him abide,
Place your trust in Him and
Safely, on His strong shoulders, He will guide,
Put your hand in His hand
And He will always be
At your side.

Julia Eva Yeardye

DIVINE PHYSICIAN

Divine Physician, Christ by God was sent
To heal our wounds and take away our pain.
To comfort us in sorrow, share our grief,
Restore to health all sinners who repent.

He came to show his Father's loving care
For all afflicted souls who mourn for sin,
To open blinded eyes and deafened ears,
Release all tortured minds from dark despair.

Recorded in Mark's Gospel, chapter five -
A raving man, frail woman, and dead child
Await his healing touch - mind to restore,
Body made whole, and lifeless form revive.

Three human souls in bondage, waiting there,
Man, woman, child - the human family.
Bondage of mind, of body, death itself.
Types of all human ills and sad despair.

Beyond all earthly help, imprisoned, they -
Await the healing touch, commanding word
To break the chains of sin, to set them free
Restore them to the true and living way.

Divine Physician, Healer of all strife,
The Saviour of his people from their sins.
King of the Jews and King of all the world,
He comes - The Prince of Peace and Lord of life.

Shirley H Ford

LIGHT OF HOPE

Time of danger, sorrow, in need of a shoulder to cry on.
It's okay to cry and to complain, how we blessed God is sweet
To put whole, our trust in Him, tell God about it,
He will hear you

Life with its ups and downs
Depressed, angry, confused, cheated.
Time after with little relief, no peace and joy within,
He's our refuge and strength he knows your inner pain
Just you ask Him, talk to Him

When hope seems to die and soul cries 'Why me?'
It's like looking through the mirror without any locks tied to
Our side and 'why?' soul cries out . . . 'Help!
Why me . . . ? Why me . . . !'
Just look up and He will be there for your need.

He cares for you, tell God about it
Be strong and of a good courage - not to be afraid,
Neither be Thou dismayed
For He knows your needs and cries
Ask for His help tell Him as He knows everything.

Honest talk with God is the first step to finding peace of mind
His hearing is open to the faintest, to cry of the most needy.
All other paths are detour to doom.
He will hear you in your times of need.
Just you ask and follow Him
'Why me . . . ? Why me . . . !'

Bless you, He loves you too, joy and patience, God of hope
Trusting Him fully.
Light of hope, lighting up your way of life.

Ranjit Singh

How My Faith Returned

(Dedicated to my Father)

I stood beside the barren oak
That once had been so fair
Wondering why nature's touch
No longer lingered there.
The answer came out of the depth
Of that old and dying tree
I lost faith in the Lord, my God
When I thought He had forsaken me.

I entered in a silent house
Where once the light had shone.
Wondering why the silence
And where the joy had gone.
I looked around that lonely room
And saw the widow there.
The question then was answered
When I saw the vacant chair.

I climbed the hill of Calvary
To look upon the Cross.
I saw the Saviour crucified
And knew the bitter loss.
In meditation's path I stood
Then I, the answer knew
The Lord God stood beside me
And my faith was born a-new.

Mary Ferguson

THE HOLY HILL

(A meditation from the Psalms)

I will lift up mine eyes unto the hills;
Even the Holy Hill of Calvary,
And I will look on Him whom I have pierced,
For there, and only there, my help shall be.

My King is set upon his Holy Hill;
(But in what grief and in what agony);
Pleading with outstretched arms and weary voice,
'My child, and what have I done unto thee?'

And I will look on Him and He will give
Himself, my craving emptiness to fill;
For He Himself is mine inheritance
And I shall rest upon His Holy hill.

Daphne Foreman

If . . .

If I could share
the burden
of your sorrow,
ease the ache
that rounds your shoulders,
take the pain
that shades your eyes
with the pallor of your grief:
then I would not feel
so impotent
as now.

Yet, in *my* sleep,
dream-filled and restless,
all I can give
are hazy prayers
and words
that hang uneasy in the air.

Sue Hansard

ULSTER'S MILLENNIUM PRAYER

The rainbows end elusive,
A commodity most rare,
And likewise peace in Ulster,
And few that seem to care.
Politicians line their pockets,
MLA to millionaire,
How many of them can we trust,
How many of them care?

This search for peace continues,
But strife deep-rooted lies,
We cling to our traditions,
We must not compromise.
The struggle will continue,
Viewpoints remain entrenched,
The hand of friendship idle,
The trigger hand still clenched.

'Twas peace on Earth the angels sang,
The truth is plain to see,
For God alone can bring us peace,
His Son our peace must be.
This peace is based on sacrifice,
Great love - a wondrous gift.
This peace from Calvary floweth,
To mend the deepest rift.

We want no fickle, fragile peace,
No peace with threat impending,
We want a peace eternal,
A peace that's never-ending.
Man's heart must be the vital source,
A heart from God above,
Self-seeking decommissioned,
A heart that's filled with love.

God grant such peace in Ulster,
God knows that's what we need,
Not based on priest or prelate,
Not based on cult or creed.
So in God's hands we leave our woes,
God's people trust and pray,
That very soon a land of peace,
God-speed that glorious day.

Stephen Shanks

BLACK FRIDAY

Two pieces of wood to make a cross
Just a few nails for a man to feel at a loss
A few jeering words from an onlooking crowd
A few sneering gestures when His head He bowed

His life all over when hardly it had begun
A life now ended of God's only Son
The confusion of this drama couldn't be denied
How many blasphemed, how many lied?

But 2,000 years later, His name lives on
This wonderful preacher God's only Son
For all true believers all was not lost
It would be His deceivers who would count the cost.

For a resurrection followed to show the way
On that awful depressing black Friday
Love will defeat hate for when hate departs
Jesus will reign in all of our hearts.

S Amphlett

HATE DESTROYS

Like a cancer, hate destroys,
others beliefs that annoy,
mutual intolerance at will,
prejudice and ignorance kill,
those that differ from you,
anyone with a variance of view,
slave to hate for any reason,
without end, senseless season,
loathing, eats away within,
with hate, you can never win,
religious and political divides,
you do not have to, to take sides,
men and women who you despise,
whether by distortions or lies,
mean you are destined to lose,
these are the choices you choose,
hatred will always be nonsense,
evil and the foolish hate, so hence,
if they hate you back, so are they,
self-destructive bigotry decays,
do accept those who are diverse,
difference means different not worse.

Christopher Higgins

Be Comforted

Autumn is the halfway house between summer and winter.
October's mist hangs heavy on the air, until the slow-dying sun
Breaks through - its weakening warmth signalling the approach
Of another season's death; and the breath of winter strengthens
With the fading of the year.

God gives life and death - His wisdom forever creating
And recreating the seasons for mankind's enjoyment.
Yet within this ebb and flow lie His deeper reasons -
A full employment of nature,
A rich deployment of resources.

In His incarnation, spring was His childhood;
In His summer He chose His disciples - taking stock
Of mankind's future in their potential.
His autumn was a time for Ministry, consolidation,
And contemplation of a momentary loss of divinity.
Winter-brief but cruel - saw His death upon the Cross.

But His winter was also our spring, His sacrifice our gain.
Each season bears the wisdom of God's word,
Each bears the simple message: I shall come back.
Be comforted; know that I am the risen Lord,
And that you, like me, shall rise again.

Jenny Proom

THE WAY

In this very air, my world,
I sense a becoming
Sending mind and spirit,
To some greater love running . . .
God's calling music awakes us inside,
from where humanities soul cannot hide.
Love through our world, by us comes the way,
Ever forward. Born as children, to the light
again, drawn.
A spiritual resurrection
into the redeeming dawn . . .
Loves revelation to each
how we respond,
by what we give, shall we reach . . .

We stand and question what are we, why?
Each tower before us, to find and climb,
for our destiny is on this living rhyme . . .

Love's unconditional spectacular power warmed hues,
emerges us now, to clearer human thoughts and views . . .
For, our spiritual transformation spins,
as lives revolve,
through loves intimate truth.
So it begins . . .

Paul Holland

PERSONAL REFLECTIONS ON ROMANS 8 V 38 & 39

For I am persuaded
That neither the circumstances of my death,
Or the traps of life,
Neither in extravagance of pleasures,
Nor temptations of occultism,
Neither now or later,
Nor any persuaders,
Neither prosperity or adversity,
Nor anything that can be named or thought of,
In the imagination or reality,
Will be able to separate me
From the love of God
That is in Christ Jesus, my Lord.

Joan Thompson

UNCLE JACK'S LAST DANCE

Uncle Jack won't come back
He's dancing up in Heaven
'He died last Monday night,'
Quavered Aunty, 'Aged 87!'

But he was only 85
As he'd admit, were he alive.
What mattered was he lived so long
No-one told Aunty she was wrong.

Their block of flats held dances
And Jack simply had to go
He flopped into the nearest chair
After gezutski! And tango!

He didn't want a fuss or cost
To sadden his relations
So in his Will he made it clear
He'd opted for cremation.

He didn't hope for afterlife -
And frankly nor do I -
But if there is an afterlife
He's dancing in the sky.

Angela Lansbury

INFORMATION

We hope you have enjoyed reading this book - and that you will continue to enjoy it in the coming years.

If you like reading and writing poetry drop us a line, or give us a call, and we'll send you a free information pack.

Write to :-

Triumph House Information
Remus House
Coltsfoot Drive
Peterborough
PE2 9JX
(01733) 898102